The Seventh Story

Us, Them, & the End of *Violence*

Gareth Higgins & Brian D. McLaren

Book design by Tyler McCabe. Find him at *tylermccabe.co*

In the spirit of the Seventh Story, we'd love you to share the message of this book as widely as possible. We would be grateful if you would point people to *theseventhstory.com* and *theporchmagazine.com*,
as well as the authors' websites: *brianmclaren.net* and *garethhiggins.net*.

ISBN 978-1-7329437-2-8

www.theseventhstory.com

Printed in Canada

Neither revolution nor reformation can ultimately change a society. Rather you must tell **a new powerful tale**, one so persuasive that it sweeps away the old myths and becomes the preferred story … one so inclusive that it gathers all the bits of our past and our present into a coherent whole, **one that even shines some light into the future** so that we can take the next step…. ***If you want to change a society, then you have to tell an alternative story***.

-Ivan Illich

Make a difference about something other than yourselves.

-Toni Morrison

1

The Story That Doesn't Work

there once was a people

let's call them
THE PEOPLE

THE PEOPLE used stories
to interpret their lives

stories of where they came from

stories of where they were going

stories that told them how to be happy

stories that told them where they were

one day, a long time ago,
one of THE PEOPLE saw another
one of THE PEOPLE holding
something
shiny

I WANT IT said one of THE PEOPLE

so he took it

when he got back home that night,
the rest of THE PEOPLE were amazed

BECAUSE I HAVE A SHINY OBJECT,
he proclaimed,
I AM IN CHARGE NOW

this first story said that the way to be
happy is to RULE OVER OTHERS

but every time that story was attempted,
people were unhappy,
because the rulers oppressed them

so a second story was invented:
LET'S OVERTHROW THE RULERS

and this story didn't rule either
because it just turned the tables,
putting new rulers in charge
and putting new people under
oppression

so another story began
in which the old revolutionaries
withdrew into their own isolated spaces
and judged the world

nothing changed

these island communities ran on the
same old stories,
some clawing their way to the top,
others trying to pull them down
and replace them at the top, and others
building shiny object factories
that filled the air with smoke and made
everyone cough —
not just the people,
but the animals,
and even the trees

meanwhile,
the DOMINATION STORY
and the ISOLATION STORY
had a business merger,
which resulted in an
experiment:

if they could get rid of the people they didn't like, who looked or sounded different, or whose customs weren't like their own, surely that would fix things?

of course that story just led to more suffering — suffering for those who were blamed and targeted and felt unsafe, and suffering for those who did the blaming and targeting, because they missed out on the gift of the rainbow they lived in a grey world

THE PEOPLE still weren't happy, and
they knew it

So they began to...
sorry I got distracted...
they began to create a new...
oh, look at that!

A shiny object! How lovely! I'd like one
of those! How can I get one?...

…a lot of years went by

THE PEOPLE tried to convince themselves that things were okay by accumulating things

toys or nations,
it was all the same to them

some of THE PEOPLE knew such things don't heal the soul, and the other old stories hadn't gone away either

THE PEOPLE kept hurting, and hurting each other

so a sixth story was created
that says if we can't find peace,
security, and happiness
by ruling the world
or overthrowing the rulers
or withdrawing into isolation
or getting rid of a minority
or by accumulating shiny objects,
then let us never forget our sorrow,
or the pain
others have caused us, for
no one has ever suffered like us

THE PEOPLE would make sure that no one would ever forget that they were the victims

that their suffering was their very identity, and that one had suffered as much as them

and if you try to tell them that others
have suffered too, they might kill you

[a long pause]

and then, something new

a poet came to town

a storyteller who knew that

the DOMINATION STORY

the REVOLUTION STORY

the ISOLATION STORY

the PURIFICATION STORY

the ACCUMULATION STORY

and the VICTIMIZATION STORY

were all destined to fail

they were destined to fail
because they invited every human being,
who is already interdependent with
every other human being, and even with
the earth itself, to pretend instead that
we are in a competition

the poet knew how to build things
like tables
where we could all sit and eat together

she taught that the people most
oppressed by the six stories should be
the most honored

she taught that our differences
aren't a reason
for shame, punishment, or exclusion,
but instead, they are marks
of what make us most lovable

she invited THE PEOPLE to join her in
forming a new community

where status would depend on service
and domination would be replaced by
equitable community

where revolution would
begin in the heart
and would lead to reconciliation,
not revenge,
transforming the process
by which we live and learn

where deadening isolation would be
replaced by rejuvenating silences

where we would learn from and
celebrate folk on the margins

where we would share not possess

and heal each other's wounds
in a new story
of power-with not power-over
of collaboration not competition
of beauty not belligerence

the poet had a radical idea

the seed of a Seventh Story
that will heal the world

the earlier six stories all claimed that the
path to peace, security, and
happiness was about WINNING

us over them

or us overthrowing them

or us staying apart from them

or us cleansing ourselves of them

or us having things that they don't

or us being more important than them
because of our competitive suffering…

but in the Seventh Story, the story of reconciliation, we still get to win, just not at anybody else's expense in the Seventh Story, human beings are not the protagonists of the world

Love is.

in the Seventh Story, humans are participants in something far bigger than being reduced to dominating others for one group's gain, or the pursuit of happiness through revolutions that replace one dominance with another, or isolation, or purity, or being a victim, or gaining possessions in the Seventh Story, humans are participants in the biggest thing that has ever happened: of the evolution of the good, of the expansion of consciousness to include the restoration and healing of all things

The Story of Love

it's a story in which some of us know
that our purpose is not merely
self-interest
but the common good

Some of Us
For All of Us

[another long pause]

they killed the poet, of course

the Seventh Story was too much to take
for people with visions limited to the
narrow circle of self

but the poet did not actually die

her story is alive,
right now

the story lives wherever someone reveals
the other stories as failures

the story lives every time someone lives
for all of us

or offers a glass of cold water to a thirsty
stranger

or a blanket for a naked person

or engages in sacred practices of
friendship, lament, and hope

the story lives wherever there are
exchanges of power and gifts between
the strong and the vulnerable,
creating community

the story lives wherever there are artistic
endeavors that show us we're not alone,
and tell us where to go next,
and remind some of us
to live for all of us

because there is no them. ✦

2

Stories, Violence, and a Two-Part Project

Brian D. McLaren

The Human Story and the Seventh Story

We've all witnessed squabbles among kids; we may even have started a few ourselves. Shouts and name-calling escalate to pushes and punches and tears.

And not just among children, of course.

The pattern repeats itself among so-called grownups who may start with threatening words, but can quickly escalate to guns and bombs.

Between playground squabbles and nuclear wars, violence

takes a thousand forms, from domestic violence to mass shootings, from petty crime to gang warfare, from drive-bys to ethnic cleansing, from suicide to geocide.

We are so used to hearing about violence, and for some of us, experiencing it, that we may never stop long enough to think that it doesn't have to be this way. Yes, conflict may be an inevitable outcome of bringing seven billion (or even just two) souls into proximity, with all our competing desires and perceptions. Yes, conflict may be a fact of life. But escalating violence does not have to be.

We can better imagine a more peaceful future if we come to terms with how violence became so much a part of our past.

Once Upon a Time...

There are many ways to tell the human story.

No single story tells us everything we need to know, so we tell more and more. Check out the bestseller list for the week, or go to the theatre, or turn on a screen or radio, or listen to a sermon: we are *homo narrator: humanity, the storytellers.*

One telling of the human story begins in a garden with a man, a woman, a tree, and a snake. In the Garden of Eden story, human beings live in an abundant environment, but they refuse to acknowledge their limits. They want to play god. Soon, brother is killing brother.

Another telling begins in a timeless, unimaginably dense singularity that explodes into a primordial big bang 13.8 billion years ago. In the aftermath of the Big Bang story, the process of evolution thrusts individuals and species into competition for survival, and the most aggressive tend to be the ones whose genes get passed on.

Both of these stories, and thousands like them, share a common purpose: to help us understand where we came from, why we're here, what's going on around us and within us, and what matters most in this mysterious, fragile, resilient life we share on this earth. And in particular, they offer an explanation for the violence that seems to follow us like a shadow wherever we go.

Stories and Violence

But consider this: if our stories successfully account for human violence, do they unintentionally justify it, normalize it, and reinforce it? Do our stories train us to think of escalating violence as inevitable, an eternal absolute of human experience? Do they train us to expect things to get worse and worse, creating the conditions for a self-fulfilling prophecy?

If we take the long view and study the statistics, it turns out that the average human is in much less danger of actually dying from violence than we were a few centuries ago. But it often doesn't feel that way. Our brains our wired for danger, so violence gets our attention like nothing else.

News media exploit our in-born violence-vigilance to win higher ratings and advertising income; politicians play on our fear of violence to win votes; and entertainers find that violence attracts viewers and sells tickets and advertising. To put it bluntly, like sex, violence sells, and a lot of us are making a handsome living on hurting and killing, which makes our relationship to violence all the more dysfunctional.

Most of us would rather not live in a kill-or-be-killed world, an enslave-or-be-enslaved world, a dominate-or-be-dominated world, an impoverish-or-be-impoverished world.

If we had a realistic chance to build a live-and-let-live world, a world of generosity and justice and neighborliness where we do to others as we'd have them do to us … we would gladly choose that option.

And that's what the Seventh Story is about. A less violent future is available. It's within reach. It lies before us like a road less traveled. But why do so few seem to choose it, so far at least? By integrating stories from anthropology, sociology, and theology, we can better understand our past and see a path to a more peaceful future.

Violence, Imitation and Desire

According to French anthropologist René Girard (1923-2015), our struggle with violence is related to a key advance in our evolution:

> At some point in our evolutionary past, our ancestors' brains made a shift in how they allocated space. Less

space was devoted to instinct so that more could be devoted to imitation.

Everything changed with that increased capacity for imitation. (Girard's word for imitation was *mimesis,* and his theory is widely known as *mimetic theory.*) Imitation enhanced human capacity for language and for the transfer of innovations, skills, and knowledge across tribes and generations. In a real sense, the brain's capacity for imitation became the basis for human culture.

But the asset of **imitation** came paired with a liability related to **desire**.

Think of a hunter-gatherer mother carrying her baby boy on her hip as she picks berries. When the baby reaches out to grab a berry for himself, he isn't simply imitating his mother's behavior; he is imitating his mother's desire for food. And similarly, when that mother points at objects and makes sounds, the child doesn't simply mimic the mother's vocalizations; he imitates the mother's desire to name and to communicate.

That's where things get interesting — and potentially violent. When the boy gets older and has a best friend his own age, imagine what happens when the best friend finds a piece of fruit. The friend's desire for the fruit stimulates the boy to imitate that desire, and instantly, he wants what his friend has. He reaches out and takes it. His mother was glad to share, but his friend may not be.

The same thing happens several years later when the boys are teenagers. The best friend feels desire for a young woman and begins to win her affections. (Of course, this also happens across the spectrum of gender and sexual orientation.) As soon as he sees how this girl is desired by his best friend, she becomes more desirable to the boy himself. And soon he may find himself flirting with his best friend's girlfriend, or trying to make his friend look bad in her eyes, or plotting to break them up somehow. He is transformed from trusted companion to a rival.

So, we depend on one another for survival. But at any moment, our companion might want what we want and become our rival — for a toy, a tool or weapon, clothing, a mate, a home, a piece of land, a means of transport, social standing, anything. This produces a deep anxiety in us as individuals and as groups. So to his observations on imitation and desire, Girard added additional insights about **rivalry** and **anxiety**.

Rivalry and Anxiety

As Girard looked for traces of this phenomenon in cultures across the world and across history, he noticed something almost universal. When rivalry and social anxiety levels reached a certain point, the point at which people feared that social stability might collapse at any moment into all-against-all violence, many societies around the world settled on a solution that was frighteningly effective and shockingly violent.

Imagine a community whose social stability is threatened. Some dominant member of the group, churning with anxiety, picks a weaker or marginal member of the group upon whom to vent his pent-up tension. As soon as he begins bullying this weaker member, he feels a little bit relieved. His sense of power is partially restored. So he keeps up the bullying. And at that moment, each bystander faces a choice. Will they imitate the leader's desire to vent their anxiety through bullying, or will they resist — thus risking that they might be the next victim?

As more and more people imitate the alpha-bully's desire, the coalition of bullies develops, and each unaffiliated member feels the excruciating tension between the deep social norm of solidarity and this spontaneous outburst of aggression that seems to be spreading among them. Eventually, teasing and mocking give way to pushing and shoving, and soon, the coalition of anxious bullies becomes a lynch mob, and eventually, the victim is either banished or murdered.

And what happens after the murder? Imagine the euphoria that spreads as a group of people who were previously divided by rivalry have been reunited through imitating one another's aggression and violence. Leadership is reestablished. Solidarity is reaffirmed. Anxieties and anger are purged. And to the degree that members feel guilt for the murder, reassurances are shared among members. "It was something we had to do," they say. "And look at us now. We're united. We're together. How could this not be good?" The victim comes to be seen, not simply as some unfortunate functionary, but as a magical or holy figure, even divine. The victim was a sacrifice whose blood had to be shed in order to reestablish the unity and health of the society.

Scapegoating and Sacrifice

Girard used two terms for this method of healing rivalry and purging anxiety and aggression through violence:

scapegoating and **sacrifice**. Scapegoating and sacrifice have been, he claimed, the proven and preferred survival strategy for human societies around the world for millennia. They have become the tried and true method for managing one of our greatest threats: intra-group rivalry. By pre-empting catastrophic violence through limited violence, scapegoating and sacrifice have become the key to solidarity and the basis of human society, making today's civilization possible.

We simultaneously depend upon the scapegoating/sacrifice mechanism and are ashamed of it, Girard hypothesized, so we seek clever ways of hiding the scandalous truth from ourselves even as we celebrate it. For example, the scandal is both concealed and revealed in many of our foundational stories — the tale of Remus and Romulus in Roman mythology, for example, or of Cain and Abel in biblical literature. Brothers kill brothers so that new civilizations can be built, and the pattern repeats again and again, from the genocide of indigenous peoples on Turtle Island to "ethnic cleansings" in places like Rwanda, Northern Ireland, the former Yugoslavia, Iraq, Syria, and Myanmar.

We ritualize this scapegoating/sacrifice mechanism in various ways. The contest of sports, for example, can be seen as a way of playing out our rivalries without actual violence, but with many of the associated behaviors: shouting, chanting, dressing up in team colors and (war)paint, declaring victors and losers, and so on. Even attending drama (or going to the movies) has elements of a ritual enactment of scapegoating and sacrifice; as viewers, we are bystanders and witnesses to violence that is often nothing short of horrific, and we leave feeling purged (at least until we become conscious of the scapegoating/sacrifice mechanism, and the need for human beings to evolve beyond it). The same could be said of the spectacle of an election cycle, where one candidate-victim after another is vilified, vanquished, and banished from the public stage, leaving one candidate who will, it is hoped, unify the divided country.

As impressive as Girard's theory was at this point, he still wasn't finished building on it. He had more to say about the process that began with imitation and desire, intensified in anxiety and rivalry, and exploded in a violent outburst of scapegoating and sacrifice.

Imagine a clan of people who live in a remote valley. Every few years, rivalries and anxieties reach such a level that the group employs the scapegoating/sacrifice mechanism. After several years, a bright young woman comes to the chief of the clan: "I have noticed that every few years, we must find and kill a victim in order to stay united. Perhaps we should choose and sacrifice this victim on a regular basis, say on the first new moon after the vernal equinox." Since the violent purgation of rivalry and anxiety clearly "works," the chief agrees and institutes a regular ritual of human sacrifice.

The bright young woman who suggested this practice would be an excellent candidate for the first priestess of the community, and in that moment, Girard suggested, both religion and government are born.Their intent, of course, was not simply to kill innocent victims. Their intent was to preclude catastrophic outbreaks of all-against-all violence born of unresolved rivalry and its associated anxiety. A little killing to avoid a lot of killing, we might say.

The priests who managed the annual ritual of human sacrifice would eventually, Girard posited, consider the possibility that animals could be ritually sacrificed instead of humans, leading to cults of animal sacrifice found in societies all around the world. This same priestly class would naturally work to reduce violence in other ways too, such as through the articulation of rules and prohibitions against actions which frequently lead to violence.

Rituals and Prohibitions

Girard continued to build his theory from its foundation in imitation and desire, to its first floor in rivalry and anxiety, to its second floor in scapegoating and sacrifice, and now, to a third floor, a pair of insights regarding **rituals** and **prohibitions**, and the development of a priestly class to maintain the whole violence-reduction edifice.

At this point, you can imagine someone, say a graduate student, coming to Girard: "Professor, have you ever applied your theory to the Bible?" And in fact, after a young adulthood as a secular French intellectual, free from religious trappings, Girard had returned to the faith of his youth. He had become astounded at the evidence Jewish and Christian texts lent to his theory.

The story begins with hunter gatherers living in an idyllic garden, nothing less than Paradise on earth. The two protagonists, Adam and Eve, are caught up in a rivalry of imitative desires with God and with one another. There is no room for this kind of rivalry in Eden, so they are banished. Their sons are similarly torn by rivalry (having to do with sacrifice). One is killed, and the other builds a city. City life intensifies violence, which God tries (unsuccessfully) to clean out with a flood (using violence to stop violence). In the story of Abraham planning to sacrifice Isaac, Girard sees the memory of replacing human sacrifice with animal sacrifice. Just as his theory predicted, a priestly class arises to manage the sacrificial system, and they impose any number of rituals and prohibitions to maintain the peace.

Peace remains fragile, however, and many episodes of scapegoating are revealed (and partially concealed) in the various books of the Hebrew Scripture, all supporting Girard's theory. But then Girard comes upon something utterly new in the Hebrew prophets and poets, who dare to say that **God does not actually desire sacrifice**, but rather **what God wants is a change in heart — compassion, humility, kindness**. This, Girard believes, marks **a turning point in human history**, a moment when a new possibility emerges. Can the nonviolent development of empathy and compassion prove even more effective at preempting violence than the violent mechanisms of scapegoating and sacrifice?

Girard's suspicions in this regard are strengthened as he reads the story of Jesus in the New Testament, clearly following the prophetic path that rejects violent sacrifice and instead pursues empathy and compassion for all people. He sees in

Jesus' crucifixion the intentional and ultimate rejection of violence, a willingness to accept torture and death rather than attempting to use violence to defeat violence. Jesus' early followers sought to imitate and embody his example of love and his rejection of violence. They were convinced that love is stronger than violence and death.

Girard concluded that the Christian religion couldn't handle Jesus' clear rejection of the scapegoat/sacrifice mechanism, and actually reversed it, reducing Jesus to a scapegoat/sacrifice needed to appease an angry God. In other words, Christians betrayed the great anthropological breakthrough offered the world through their founder. The religion rebuilt what its founder actually sought to tear down: a culture based on violence.

Late in life, Girard became despondent. **Human societies have evolved too fast technologically and too slow morally**, he felt. We have invented weapons so disastrous that if we use them, the results will be suicidal. But we have not yet developed an alternative way of dealing with the problem of imitation and desire. Perhaps empathy and compassion could have become as contagious as rivalry and violence, but it was too late, Girard concluded. We missed our chance, and now we are stuck in hopeless cycles of violence that will keep us battling to the end.

Growing numbers of us see great value in Girard's theory, but we don't share his despair. We see how negative imitation has trapped people in cycles of violence, and we are eager to model nonviolent living and leadership for positive imitation. We believe that many of our neighbors haven't yet chosen a nonviolent story because their imaginations are still held captive by stories of domination and fear, stories that have dominated human societies for thousands of generations.

Blinded by Violence

One specific source of violence has plagued human societies from one generation to the next: male aggressiveness. Men who were not initiated into integrating or managing their aggression, fueled by androgen, testosterone, and social conditioning, have expressed their aggression in their families as tyrants who often traumatized their spouses and children. In their communities, they became violent criminals, bullies, gang leaders and members, terrorists and violent religious extremists, corporate bosses who exploited others for their own profit, and violent chiefs, governors, princes, kings, dictators, and emperors. Of course, women have been violent players in these sad stories too, but in human history so far, men have taken the lead when it comes to violent conflict, and women and children have often been caught in the crossfire.

Many millennia ago, human societies devised a response to this problem of male aggressiveness. They elevated one alpha male to a position of power above all the beta and gamma males (and all the women, too), creating hierarchies of dominance and submission. It was a deal: in exchange for keeping all the unruly men under control, a dominant father figure would be rewarded with extra power, privilege, prestige, and perks, including financial and sexual perks.

What kind of man would be elevated to such a position? In order to intimidate any potential rival into submission, he must be willing to deploy violence faster and more ruthlessly than anyone else. And he must be willing to "display," not just once, but constantly — to remind all potential upstarts of his physical prowess, his sexual prowess, and his financial prowess, so they'll remember just who the alpha male is. To defeat violence, the alpha male will concentrate violence, and by fighting violence with violence, he promises peace.

Patriarchy and Politics

The name for this system is patriarchy. It can exist in a family, a clan, a tribe, a nation, or an empire. Beginning about five centuries ago, European patriarchs (popes, kings, and their cronies) extended their patriarchal regimes globally, so that since the colonial period, global patriarchy has expressed itself as white Christian male supremacy for much of the world.

Since patriarchs inevitably age, weaken, and die, transitions must happen each generation. In the past, family succession was the norm, with the first-born son inheriting the patriarchal throne. But primogeniture didn't always work well, so transitions were often bloody.

In response, many societies developed a kinder and gentler form of patriarchy called democracy, which gave men the right to vote to elect their next patriarchs. As a result, patriarchs could rise to power using displays of words, wealth, and charm rather than weapons.

Of course, white men were still running the show, but that began to change slowly but significantly in the late 19th and

20th centuries. In the US, for example, black men were given the right to vote in 1870, although that right was severely curtailed in many states through Jim Crow laws. Gradually, and through a long struggle, some women won the right to vote fifty years later, in 1920. It wasn't until 1924 that Native Americans won that right, although some states still refused to enfranchise them until 1957. The Voting Rights Act of 1965 was intended to democratize voting more fully, yet still today, powerful white men in many states use gerrymandering and other techniques of voter suppression to retain their advantage.

More recently, women were chosen as vice presidential running mates in 1984, 2008, and 2016. Such a move kept the patriarch in the lead, but acknowledged the rising power of women. Then in 2016, women ran for president in both party primaries, and for the first time, a woman won a majority of votes to lead the nation.

As more women are elected to public office, it signals far more than breaking a "glass ceiling." It signals a tipping point in a global shift beyond patriarchy. We stand, we might say, on the threshold of a post-patriarchal culture, a culture that seeks new qualities in leaders, and is open to building peace and security in new, nonviolent ways.

There are other ways, it turns out, to manage male aggressiveness: through cultural, religious, and professional norms, through education and laws, and through effective modeling by both female and male leaders. Post-patriarchal leaders can embody nonviolent qualities such as curiosity, humility, honesty, compassion, moral integrity, long-range thinking, systems thinking, "both/and" or non-dual thinking, nonviolence, exemplary service, generosity, and collaboration.

In this way, we stand at the threshold of not just another story, but a new kind of story, a new chapter in the evolution of *homo narrator.*

Regression to Old Stories

But growth and progress, while possible, are not inevitable. Regression to patriarchal violence remains an option, especially in times of anxiety.

One one level, we might say that people are less likely to risk something new when they are under stress, the "devil you know" being preferable to the one you don't. So the risk of moving farther in a post-patriarchal direction sometimes proves too much for stressed-out electorates. Made chronically anxious through a mix of real threats and media-generated anxieties, voters around the world remain vulnerable to the next patriarchal display of an authoritarian strongman.

Violent Religion

Meanwhile, patriarchal men keep finding ways both subtle and obvious to reassert their dominance. We might expect sexual braggadocio and "kick-ass attitudes" to turn off religious people, but actually, traditional religion consistently reinforces the primal lure of violent patriarchy. After all, God in traditional monotheism is most commonly imaged as a Zeus-like super-patriarch, ready to smite with violence those who defy his (the pronoun fits) omnipotence. With an all-powerful patriarch at the top of the great chain of being, threatening the rebellious with the ultimate violence of eternal conscious torture, the whole universe is rendered eternally patriarchal.

Strong-man personas and patterns of toxic male demagoguery feel less threatening, more familiar, and even strangely comforting to believers in a patriarchal universe. Their patriarchal religious orientation renders these traditional believers more ready to forgive or ignore a bit of sexual assault, punch-him-in-the-face pugilism, racial innuendo, and unself-conscious arrogance, as long as their leaders play the familiar patriarchal role. After all, patriarchal boys will be boys, whether they're boy presidents, governors, supreme court nominees, senators, bishops, priests, or pastors.

A New Kind of Faith

This "boys will be boys" cliché, of course, is a self-perpetuating myth. And while organized religion remains the last bastion of patriarchy in many parts of the world, growing numbers of forward-leaning Jews, Muslims, Christians, Hindus, Sikhs, Buddhists, and others are quickly evolving beyond patriarchy and the violence and injustice it entails.

For example, progressive Christians no longer see Christmas as the birth of a deified alpha male who plays by the same old set of patriarchal rules. Instead, Christmas celebrates a poor, young woman giving birth to an omega male, a kind, humble, and nonviolent man who teaches and embodies a new post-patriarchal understanding of God, the universe, masculinity, and human society.

Now Jesus' core message of the kingdom of God, along with his use of the word *Abba* or "Father" for God, may at first seem like a reinforcement of patriarchal domination. But a closer examination of Jesus' life and teaching show that Jesus came to subvert all stories of violence and harm, not repeat them.

> Instead of patriarchal stories of **domination**, he taught and embodied service, reconciliation, and self-giving.
>
> Instead of stories of violent **revolution or revenge** on the one hand or compliant submission on the other, he taught and modeled transformative nonviolent resistance.
>
> Instead of the **purification** stories of scapegoating or ethnic cleansing, he encountered and engaged the other with respect, welcome, neighborliness, and mutuality.
>
> Instead of inhabiting a competitive story of **accumulation**, he advocated stewardship, generosity, sharing and a vision of abundance for all.

> Instead of advocating escapist stories of **isolation**, he sent his followers into the world to be agents of positive change, like salt, light, and yeast.
>
> And instead of leaving the oppressed in stories of **victimization**, he empowered them with a vision of faith, hope, and love that could change the world.

The patriarchal spirit, we might say, is an unholy spirit of conquest, control, and intimidation, exclusion, privilege, and entitlement, theft, violence, and destruction. But the holy Spirit of God as embodied by Jesus bears the nonviolent fruit of love, joy, and peace; patience, kindness, and gentleness; and faithfulness, generosity, and self control.

When religious people retreat into old stories of patriarchal authoritarianism, they are saying, in effect, "We have no king but Caesar." The only leadership they will recognize and follow is the broad, old, well-worn highway of authoritarian patriarchy.

But we advocate a new path, a new story, a new way of life, in which love, not violence, is the protagonist.

A New Logic, A New Story

The Greek philosopher Heraclitus said that the logos or deepest logic of the world is *polemos* — war, struggle, conflict. He was right. That has indeed been the dominant human logic or story for thousands of years.

But in a world of nuclear, biological, and chemical weapons, stories that claim violence can defeat violence can never be the solution. They are the heart of the problem.

That's why we need social and spiritual visionaries who help liberate our imaginations. From the Buddha and Isaiah to Jesus and Muhammad, our seminal religious leaders have challenged us to imagine a less violent world. In more modern times, theologians like Walter Wink and Desmond Tutu, anthropologists and social scientists like Girard and Erica Chenoweth, and social/spiritual activists like Dorothy Day, Gandhi, and Dr. King have challenged our shades-of-gray narratives of violence and helped us envision a full-color world where differences can inspire connection, affection, and mutuality rather than fear, division, and death.

Through the influence of these social and spiritual

visionaries, the hearts of more and more children, young people, adults, and senior citizens are yearning for a new story, a story of love rather than hate, of creativity rather than destruction, of win-win cooperation rather than win-lose competition, of peace-craft rather than warcraft.

They are waiting for a new story to explore, inhabit, and tell.

They are ready to embark on a project with two interrelated elements:

1. To unmask the deceptive power of violence, to remove its magic sheen, and to show it for what it really is: a vicious, addictive cycle that creates a temporary euphoria, temporary order, and temporary unity, but in the long run, leads in a downward spiral ending in civilizational suicide.

2. To explore the regenerative power of a seventh story, a story of liberation, reconciliation, creativity, and peace. We want to stop telling stories that make heroes of violent people and instead celebrate nonviolent examples whose lives inspire us all to imitate their compassion, kindness, understanding, wisdom, and willingness to suffer for the truth rather than make others suffer. These positive examples will help us leave old stories behind and choose a

better human story for a better human future.
Salman Rushdie said it well: "Those who do not have power over the story that dominates their lives — the power to retell it, rethink it, deconstruct it, joke about it, and change it as times change — truly are powerless, because they cannot think new thoughts."

If you hear this new story, this seventh story deeper and higher and wider than our typical stories of violence, suddenly your options expand, new thoughts spring up, and a better way of life is possible. ✦

Why do we hurt each other?

If René Girard is right, it's because we have been taught to believe that peace and security will come through having what we believe others want; and that when our boundaries are challenged, we must harm or even kill those who would get between us and our stuff. We have defined belonging not by what we cherish and love and share, but by whom we exclude and how we can hold onto what we have taken.

My childhood in northern Ireland was catechized by violence — by paramilitary groups, by the state, circumscribing my sense of safety and belonging. Each side blamed only the other, and sought to entirely eradicate their opponent's power, "cleansing" the land for a future utopian dream, of a “free” Ireland or “saved” Ulster. Violence begat violence, until the truth became obvious: our peace could not come at the price of one side being defeated. Only some form of nonviolent compromise, in which everyone’s needs were equally valued, could lift us out of the cycle.

The killing happened in the first place because we were living out *the myth of redemptive violence*, the archetypal story that says we can bring order out of chaos through lethal force. This term, coined by the magnificent theologian and activist Walter Wink, arose out of studies of the stories human beings use to describe our experience of the world, and how those stories themselves shape our experience of reality. What Walter discovered was that the story we tell at the very foundation of our narratives is that violence is at the foundation of the world.

It is our creation myth.

The oldest known surviving work of literature, the *Epic of Gilgamesh*, includes a story about the origins of human beings that would not be out of place in the goriest of fantasy action cinema. Gilgamesh includes the creation myth of the ancient Babylonians — now known as the people of Iraq, who, among other things, invented civilization. The story, with some contemporary remixing, goes something like this:

before there was anything,
there was nothing

and out of that nothing emerged
two gods

male and female

and for eons, the two gods were friends
and lovers

but eventually, they became lonely

being surrounded by nothing will do
that do you

so they decided to have kids

kid gods

who arrived in great number
and pleased them

they were a family now

it worked well
for a few millenia

kids playing,
parents caring,
everyone having fun

but after a few more eons had passed,
Mom and Dad were tired

irritated, even

for their kids, despite (or perhaps due to)
being deities, made far too much noise

so Mom and Dad pondered

but not for too long
because the kids were making
FAR TOO MUCH NOISE

there was only one thing to be done

kill the kids

but the kids were quicker

they were fans of Louis Armstrong, and had heard him sing, "They'll learn much more than I'll ever know"

so they overpowered Dad god
and killed him

Mom escaped

(at which point an ancient literary
scholar might pop and note,
"Which is interesting, because this
means the earliest written-down
creation myth ascribes more power to
the female than the male; matriarchy
precedes patriarchy"

thank you, ancient literary scholar)

so the kids re-grouped

“What are we going to do?” they cried

the strongest kid god, the edgiest one,
the one I imagine sitting at the back of
the room like Quint in *Jaws*, scratching
his fingernails down the chalkboard to
get their attention, spoke

“I’ll do it. For a price.”

"Whatever it takes, brother."

"I'll do it. If you make me supreme ruler of the universe."

"Whatever it takes."

so the strongest kid prepared his armory

a wine sack filled with poison gas
a bow and arrow
and a smile

he wouldn't want to frighten her, you
know?

finding his mother somewhere in the
distant reaches of the cosmos,
he approached gently

"Hi, Mom"

"Hello, son. Are you going to hurt me?"

"No, of course not. I just want to give
you a kiss."

she smiled, relieved that everything
would be okay

sneakily he turned, and gulped a
mouthful of the poison gas

kissing her, he blew the gas into her
mouth

the shock caused her to swallow

she barely managed to squeeze out the
cry
"What have you done?"
before the effects of the gas paralyzed
her vocal chords

her neck burned
her stomach filled
her belly distended

she jerked and vibrated at a hundred
miles an hour, and began to spin in space

her son, the Supreme Ruler of the Universe-elect, stood on an asteroid for leverage, and precisely aimed his arrow

let go

the arrow flew
the arrow of time
the arrow of meaning
the arrow of destruction and of
recreation
the first strategic act of lethal force
the foundation of all violence

it landed dead-center in her stomach

she felt the first prick, and nothing
more, before she exploded

flesh and bone and entrails were thrust
out beyond their belonging

floating there,
the son gathered himself, relieved

there was work to do

he took the parts of his mother
and began to put them together

when he was done, there was a universe

and planets

and people

people made from the blood and guts of
a murdered mother god

order out of chaos,
brought about by ultimate force

we were made from murder

*

Stories matter.

We know that to survive, humans need four things: food, water, air, and protection from the elements.

But beyond four walls and a roof, we seek a deeper shelter. Along with meeting our physical needs, every ordinary life, like yours and mine, seeks to find, and make, meaning. The search for meaning is nothing more than the pursuit of happiness and security; and the pursuit of happiness and security is really the search for meaning, because when we find true meaning in life, including the way meaning manifests as belonging to a community and a place, happiness and security take care of themselves. From the earliest moments of our lives, we adopt and adapt lenses through which we see the world, handed down by family, community, and cultural traditions. We are told that these will both show us what we want and how to get it. In other words, they will shelter us. The path toward or away from shelter shows up in the systems of our everyday lives:

Family and cultural practices.

Education.

Artistic and cultural expression.

Political and legislative boundaries.

Economic or gift exchange.

Community organizing and social movements.

Religious and spiritual transformation.

These are also the lenses through which we experience life generally, and they do not exist in isolation from each other. Indeed, they are all gathered in one larger circle, each with a part to play, but none bigger than the circle itself.

The circle is not religion, nor philosophy, nor ethics, nor politics, nor economics, nor science, nor aesthetics, although it's hard to imagine the circle without any of these.

The circle is **storytelling**, and there is nothing more powerful.

The myth of redemptive violence is a foundational story of our times. The evidence is simple, and clear: we act like we believe it, when we seek to bring order out of chaos through force. The evidence for why this belief is wrong is simple, and clear: observable reality disproves it. Killing does not cleanse. Violence does not bring peace. We don't ultimately feel better, or find shelter by destroying someone else's life, or even merely assassinating their character. Wars beget wars until one party is overwhelmed, or decides to stop. Nobody wins. We need a new story.

Of course, it is not really "new" — we use "new story" in similar way to Charles Eisenstein, who means it as "new for modern civilization as a guiding narrative"; old ideas can be better than the more recent ones; and some old ideas have not so much failed but never been properly attempted.

Perhaps even more exciting: some good old ideas are ready to come to life like never before. Now, if industrial societies began to live according to the principles of reconciliation and connection with self, others, the earth, and love itself — well, that would be a new story indeed. So what we need is *another* story, one so ancient and usually misunderstood that it may seem entirely new.

*

We comprehend...that nuclear power is a real danger for mankind, that overcrowding of the planet is the greatest danger of all.

We have understood that the destruction of the environment is another enormous danger.

But I truly believe that the lack of adequate imagery is a danger of the same magnitude. It is as serious a defect as being without memory.

What have we done to our images?

What have we done to our embarrassed landscapes?

I have said this before and will repeat it again as long as I am able to talk: if we do not develop adequate images we will die out like dinosaurs.

–*Werner Herzog*

My friend Colin, an architect, and kind of a mystic, says that the purpose of his craft is to help people live better. There's beautiful simplicity, but also enormous gravity in that statement. Just imagine if every public building, city park, urban transportation hub, and home were constructed with the flourishing of humanity — in community or solitude — in mind. Sometimes this is already the case, and we know it when we see it. Our minds and hearts feel more free, we breathe more easily, we are inspired to create things — whether they be new thoughts of something hopeful, or friendships with strangers, or projects that will bring the energy of transformation yet still into the lives of others.

If architecture, manifested at its highest purpose, helps us live better, then it is also easy to spot architecture that is divorced from this purpose. In our internal impressions of a building or other space made to function purely within the boundaries of current economic mythology — especially buildings made to house the so-called "making" of money — the color of hope only rarely reveals itself. Instead we are touched by melancholy, weighed down by drudgery, even compelled by the urge to get away. But when we see the shaping of a space whose stewards seem to have known that human kindness is more important than the free market, that poetry and breathing matter beyond bank balances and competition (a concert hall designed for the purest reflection of sound, a playground where the toys blend in with the trees, a train station where the transition from one place and way of being to another has been honored as a spiritual act), we know that it is possible to always be coming home.

This is not just true for architecture, but for all art. All stories, actually. So when occasions arise to speak to the well-worn question of the greatest stories ever told, my criteria may differ from the most popular view. Instead of *greatest,* what about *most humane* or *transformative* or *courageous?* What about movies or books or television shows or pieces of music that made me laugh to the point of tears as I felt more part of the human race, or stories that led to healing social change, or stories that made me want to grow up?

I've spent more time with cinema than other art forms, so it's from movies that I draw most of my examples, but what I say here applies to any kind of storytelling. Literature, journalism, television, music, politics, religion, video games, activism, and everyday ordinary conversation all embody stories that have the power to heal or destroy. Movies, like all stories, have engaged moral and cultural questions since they began. Even the notional very first movie — the Lumière Brothers' silent short, "Workers Leaving the

Factory," (in which, surprise surprise, workers leave a factory) — invites such questions. Who are these people? What is the factory? What are the conditions in which the workers find themselves? Who are we to be recording them? Early movies were marketed as window box entertainments, like circus acts or roller coasters, but the potential of the medium to explore and help make sense of real life soon revealed itself. The best-known early examples are probably Charlie Chaplin's silent comedies of the underclass, which unfolded tales of poverty, opening up the audience either to compassion for the oppressed, or self-recognition as a target of economic injustice.

The movies have always been sources of solace and provocation across genres:

The battlefield epics *All Quiet on the West Front, Paths of Glory, Come and See,* and *The Thin Red Line* confront audiences with the futility of war.

Imaginative explorations of family and community life like *Fanny and Alexander, Paris, Texas,* and *Smoke* invite us to take love more seriously than we take ourselves.

Evocations of the inner life and outer expression like *Andrei*

Rublev, the *Three Colors Trilogy*, and *Yi-Yi* wonder aloud about ambition, power, and the undeniability of spiritual transcendence.

We dance (because dancing is great and heals the world!) with Gene Kelly in *Singin' in the Rain*, we laugh and learn about managing our various personas with Bing-Bong in *Inside Out*, and we see the journey toward spiritual maturity in *Groundhog Day*.

And films like *La Règle du Jeu*, *Munich*, *The Village*, *Of Gods and Men*, *Lone Star*, *Do the Right Thing* and *The Great Beauty* investigate the relationship between individuals and history, and nudge us toward the hope that we might learn something from the past.

There are thousands more where those came from — a place where the mind of an artist organized other artists in community to enter into the highest standards of craft, and the most humane vision of the world, to produce a work of surpassing beauty. Now while it's important to know that while a great film helps us live better, this doesn't mean a film needs to be happy or "safe" to be great. That would deny greatness to Greek tragedy, *King Lear*, and *Schindler's List* alike. Can the art of movie-making be an act of social justice? Of course it can: the Polish film *A Short Film About Killing* was instrumental in the abolition of the death penalty there; *Thelma & Louise* upended the portrayal of women as second class citizens; Michael Moore's films have been a mirror to injustice (and his *Where to Invade Next* proposes solutions); the very fact that the Iranian director Jafar Panahi, threatened by his own government, makes films is a challenge to political repression; the astonishing *The Act of Killing* both memorializes genocide victims and has some of those responsible begin to take on the burden of their own violence.

To ask whether or not cinema can be dangerous is to state the obvious. Stories shape our lives, and the limits of what we believe to be possible or preferable. Movies are among the most powerful story delivery mechanisms the world has ever seen, and with power comes not only the potential to heal, but the risk of danger. And while they may be overtaken by social media, video games, and news-infotainment, there's something unique about how we receive and process movie images and stories.

To take just one aspect that seems ubiquitous, the way the stories we tell deal with violence is enormously important. We are always posed a simple question: do our stories tell the truth about violence? Do we see the impact of a killing, not just in gore but the ripple effect of trauma and loss (not to mention a plausible portrayal of what leads people to kill in the first place)? Is violence in our stories portrayed proportionately? Research shows that the world appears to be getting less violent, but when we tell stories, are we tuned into the reality that one of the factors why violence reduces is when people are encouraged to empathize with "enemies," and to see lethal force as a last resort? Is the movie or book or political speech challenging, transcending, or simply reinforcing or even worshipping the belief that violence brings order out of chaos? (If you want to define paradox, sit down with these questions after a triple bill of *The Godfather Part II*, *Kill Bill*, and *Transformers: Revenge of the Fallen*. One is a tragedy revealing the repeating damage that violence does even to those who commit it, one is nationalistic propaganda for the war on terror, and one is either a cartoonish, dehumanized celebration of horrific killing, or a hymn to motherhood. The question may be simple, but the answer isn't.)

We're in this welcome cultural moment where the underrepresentation of women and people of color in the stories we tell in public is being challenged. Choosing to diversify what we watch, read, or listen to (especially stories told from the perspective of someone other than white men) would be a step toward embracing the best of this extraordinary, exquisite medium of storytelling and image revelation.

In case some may say that the central idea here fails to account for the aesthetics and technical craft of stories, let me be clear:

For me, it's simple: the purpose of storytelling — as an *art-form*, and as a communal and individual experience — is to help us live better.

The best stories help us understand more of who we are, and how to transcend our brokenness without excluding our shadows. My definition of a great story?

A great story is what results when humanizing wisdom and grace, and technical and aesthetic craft operating at their highest frequencies kiss each other.

What the distinguished peace theorist and activist John Paul Lederach calls "the moral imagination" with which artists dance can expand the possibilities of violence reduction and healing, or reinforce the terms on which violence seeks to justify itself. This is the artist's highest calling — whether we find ourselves in a situation of escalating dehumanization, or one in which violence is already decreasing. If our task as storytellers is to tell the truth in a way that escalates humanization, and if part of the truth is that violence isn't entertaining, and that stories and images can heal or destroy, then what, indeed, are the greatest stories ever told?

*

Long ago, when we first realized that it was nice to have stuff, and that other folk might want to take our stuff away, even if we didn't realize that the reason we wanted stuff in the first place was that other folk also had stuff, what seemed most natural was to find ways to keep the stuff, and prevent others getting it. We defined peace as keeping "our" stuff, while making sure "they" have less. Over time, humans have synthesized six primary stories as ways of organizing our lives so that we get to hold onto "our" stuff.

The first story that evolved to handle the task was the **domination** story: "we" would rule over "them."

This oppression provoked the emergence of a **revolution** story, often expressing itself as revenge, one form of domination replaced with another.

Another typical manifestation was the **purification** story, in which all the troubles of a powerful group were blamed on a minority, who would be excluded or even exterminated.

The pain was so great that some people began to define themselves by what they had suffered, a **victimization** story, which some aggressively maintained.

Others simply withdrew, believing in the righteousness of their own group, called to an **isolation** story in a wilderness or a promised land, where the domination cycle would begin over again.

And the people who perhaps thought themselves to be the smartest of all just retreated into trying to possess as much as they could: living by an **accumulation** story which pretended that happiness comes from having stuff, and doing our best to keep it.

Back to square one. And repeat:

—Empires, Roman, British, Intergalactic, or those based on extracting resources from the land without thought of sustainability, or in institutions like schools and businesses where people were ruled rather than collaborated with.

—Revolutions that sought to replace one oppressive order with another variation of power-over rather than power-with, and which exacted the ultimate punishment on the old leaders, denying the humanity of those who had done it to "us", thereby becoming just like "them."

—Purifications by nationalism and the shadow side of religion, projecting enemies onto anyone whose differences did not accord with a more dominant view.

—People living as nothing more than victims, unable to find repair for their experience of suffering (or perhaps never offered it), instead treasuring it, defending it, threatening or hurting those who proposed an alternative perspective, or invited healing. Entire nations have been built on the victimization story told by settlers, so powerful a story that it blinded them to the enslavement and genocide they enacted to secure what they believed was freedom.

—And of course there have been communities who have withdrawn into isolation, a holy remnant, the elite, the chosen fleeing the corrupt. Even today, some folk prepare for such a future.

—Meanwhile some people have come to the conclusion that consuming more things will keep us safe and happy; the idea that humans must hold onto what we possess, or even that we can possess things in the first place, rather than steward them for the common good, is merely another lie that we've bought.

*

We call these six the "default-oppositional" stories, and they have touched us all. Many of us were taught some variation of them as if it were the natural order of things to dominate, revolt, purify, isolate, define ourselves as victims, or accumulate for its own sake. We may even have consciously structured our lives around one or more of these stories. Each is rooted in a desire that is completely natural, and good: the pursuit of happiness, security, peace, *meaning*.

Yet each fails to achieve any of those things, because each depends on a false premise: that on earth, among humans, there is "us" and there is "them." The six stories all depend on scapegoating others, and defining happiness on the basis of what "we" can get for "ourselves."

The domination story invites us to rule over them.

The violent revolution story demands that we overthrow oppressors even if it kills them, and dominate them in return.

The purification story names, blames, shames, excludes, and sometimes eradicates minorities.

The victimization story alienates us and invites us to self-harm by defining "our" suffering as greater than "theirs," perpetuating violence by demanding vengeance.

The isolation story causes us to forfeit the gifts of the rainbow by withdrawing from community.

The accumulation story deadens our souls by defining our happiness on the basis of the "things" we "own," and causes others to suffer by withholding the bread we have from those who need it.

Such stories are everywhere. Each of us has been wooed, or coerced, or willingly gone along with them. And upon such stories we have built a world of "us" and "them."

Us over them.

Us versus them.

Us versus some of us.

Us in spite of them.

Us away from them.

Us competing with them to get more "stuff."

Can you see how a world built on such stories can only be one in which we fight each other? Can you see how, in such a world, peace is impossible?

Can you see how, now that humans have the power to wipe ourselves out, we need another story?

*

There is a Seventh Story.

It is evoked in many wisdom traditions, but in the one that Brian and I know best, it emerged about 2,000 years ago, when a poet-craftsman started teaching a bunch of Middle Eastern peasants the meaning of love. The poet radically interrupted the six stories, saying that instead of getting stuff and keeping others from getting stuff, you can't actually possess stuff for yourself alone in the first place. Instead of building walls, you are invited to show the same kindness toward your neighbor as you would want them to show to you, to celebrate his joys, to grieve her losses. Even more provocative: instead of defeating enemies, you are asked to love them.

And what is love? *To extend oneself for the purpose of nurturing one's own or another's spiritual growth* (M. Scott Peck). In other words, instead of asking what's in it for me, to see "me" as part of one enormous "us", that includes not just people, but the earth, and even love itself.

We call this **the reconciliation-liberation story.**

The most revolutionary, if you will, part of the Seventh Story — the part that makes it of an entirely different character than the six — is this: in each of the six stories, humans are masters of "our" domain, the world is divided into "us" and "them," and the purpose of life is to be a selfish economic unit, producing bounty to keep for yourself and your group.

The six stories are all based on reacting to other people's desire; they invite separation at best, and violence at worst; and they seek to avoid suffering. They ultimately portray human beings as depraved, untrustable, unlovable. Pawns in a war story, run by uncontrollable demons. And in a world where we have the power to destroy ourselves, they are evolutionarily inappropriate.

But in the Seventh Story, human beings are not the protagonists.

Love is.

We are not masters of "our" domain, but partners in the evolution of goodness. As Girard wrote, "What Jesus invites us to imitate is his own desire, the spirit that directs him toward the goal on which his intention is fixed: to resemble [love] as much as possible."

Instead of reacting to other people's desire, we would be immersed in hopeful practice toward the common good. Invited to connection, not separation. Invited to choose to participate in the inevitable suffering that life will bring, rather than avoiding it by displacing it onto others. To see ourselves as beautiful, worthy of trust, lovable. Participants in a great play about the evolution of the story of love. To be friends, not enemies, no matter what anybody else is doing. Not us versus them.

Instead: some of us for all of us.

*

The first thing I remember is looking under the car to see if there was a bomb there. The next thing I remember is more stories of death, and more, and more, and more. You would think, looking back, that killing was the only thing that happened in the northern Ireland of my childhood. But it wasn't. We were living through the ugly closing stages of a violent civil conflict that was eight hundred years in the making. The wounds of neighbor pitted against neighbor are real, and none of the killing was worth it. But it was the end of something, not the beginning. Seen up close and personal, it could feel like we were living in hell. But looked at from a distance, there was beauty, too.

The Giant's Causeway. Seapark. Donaghadee. The Craigantlet hills. Seamus Heaney. Open fire places. Van Morrison. Mairead Maguire. Glenlyon Park. The People.

And the attempts made over decades to resolve the conflict nonviolently finally paid off. Former sworn enemies now accept the principle of sharing power. Moves continue to help people make peace with the past. We promise to never do such horror to each other again. And as we seek to integrate the wounds and the fear with the community and the healing, we understand that the key is to try to tell the story in a way that produces more light than heat. The same is true, wherever you are. Stories that increase a sense of threat end up producing more violence. Most of these stories also happen to be inaccurate. Stories that decrease a sense of threat end up reducing violence. Most of these stories also happen to be true.

*

The key here is to tell the story truthfully — that the trend is toward reduced violence and increased peace, but this has occurred only because human beings have challenged codes and practices that were considered unchangeable. The mass barbarism of execution for public entertainment, the elitist madness of resolving wounded honor by duels, the horrific subjugation and even killing of people with physical differences because they were believed to be worthless all once seemed normal. The most ordinary of people responded to their circumstances by deciding to act, and stop what once had seemed immovable, but now could no longer be tolerated. We will do the same, not by waiting on social forces to do the work for us, for they are not the puppeteers of history, but invitations to action.

As Rabbi Michael Lerner says, Martin Luther King is not known for a speech entitled "I have a complaint." Of course he spoke against the injustices of his time (chief among them what he called the evil triplets of racism, militarism, and materialism), but he also outlined a vision to overcome them. No longer willing to tolerate dehumanization, he and the people he led rose up, challenging the old order, but instead of merely replacing one form of domination with another, they offered a bridge to restoration.

Every generation has the opportunity to become sensitized to the injustice whose time has come. For ours it might be capital punishment, or human trafficking, or the dehumanization of people on account of who they love, or white supremacy in civic institutions, or the encroachment of the national security state. For you, it may be the more transcendent evils of earth abuse, the systematic exclusion of people on grounds of the money they don't have, or the trading practices that deliver cheap products to Westerners while keeping the hands that make them tied to a wheel of exhaustion and endless dissatisfaction (or worse) whose time has come. For me, it is our culture's addiction to the story that violence resolves conflict. Our real religion is the god of violence, the demonic notion that killing can create things. Yet violence is never constructive, even in the extremely limited circumstances where it may be arguably necessary.

*

Violence doesn't create anything.

That's a radioactive statement — when I say it in certain circles, the negative reaction is swift and unambiguous. It's ironic that conversation about reducing violence often results in a fight. But the outcome of even that fight proves the point — violence doesn't create anything. Except suffering, of course.

People react to this suggestion with such intense opposition for a number of reasons. We have been taught from the earliest age the opposite: that violence works. We have been inculcated through our national and community rituals that violent sacrifice is noble, and that our "freedoms" were not only secured by the deaths of our forebears (and the killing they carried out), but that such death and killing was *the only way it could have happened.* And we have been nurtured into a catechism of fearing the world, so that we must always have violence as a recourse, because we never know when they are going to target us. It's perfectly reasonable, if such premises were true, to live fearful and ready to kill.

But the premises are false.

The suffering caused by violence, even in the most noble of causes, does not end when the shooting stops. The First World War produced a divided Baltic people, meaning that their grandchildren and great-grandchildren would perpetrate or suffer genocide seventy years later. The vengeance-fueled response to Germany after that war laid the foundations for the rise of Nazism. The "resolution" of the Second World War allowed Stalin to kill more people than Hitler. The refusal of political opponents to talk to each other in northern Ireland perpetuated the terms of our conflict for decades, eventually killing nearly 4,000, and physically injuring 43,000 people in a place with a population around the same size as Manhattan. And when the talking started, the killing radically reduced, and has been reducing ever since we started to see our destinies as more mutual than respective.

The sacrifices which gained our freedom — whatever "freedom" may be — may indeed have been sacrifices, and some of them were certainly noble. But the idea that only violence cleanses the nation and makes it free is comprehensively disproven in the historical fact that nonviolent revolutions are both more sustained, and produce more democracy than violent attempts at political change. The sacrifice of talking to the person who killed your mother, so that they can face and begin to make amends for the damage they caused; the sacrifice of forgoing revenge in exchange for the common good, so we can end the cycle of violence; the sacrifice of not getting everything you want so that most of us can get *something*: these are the sacrifices that work.

The threat of the world today is lied about every time you open your computer or switch on your phone. Terror lives in your pocket, on a device that does not differentiate between wisdom, information, propaganda, and deceit. The good news is that you can learn more than ever before, connect quicker, and heal yourself (some of the world's great healers and healing techniques are mobile apps). The challenge — and the invitation — is that you need to learn how to edit what you're seeing. No one else will do that for you; indeed, it is in the interests of the military-industrial-entertainment-gossip-complex that you stay unconscious, and click on as many links as possible.

The current global crisis is a crisis of storytelling. We have become possessed by the myth of redemptive violence, manifesting through six old stories that keep us apart, cause more suffering by attempting to avoid it, and simply do not work. Telling the story in those ways exaggerates fear, and violence will increase. The redemption of the myth of redemptive violence is not to destroy it by beating the "bad guys" at their own game.

No.

The way to redeem the myth of redemptive violence is to de-story it: to refuse to play the game at all. To invent a new game. To tell the story in a new way that decreases fear, so violence will reduce.

It's not a sin to feel fear; in fact, it's quite natural, given both our evolutionary past as the chase targets of saber tooth tigers and the contemporary immersive (dis)information culture that implies such beasts are still waiting round every corner. Many of us also have stories of real suffering from our own personal narratives, and the way we have learned to remember and talk about these stories keeps us reliving the trauma, endlessly looking for a way out, but never finding it, because as self-perceived victims, we begin from the premise that there is nothing we can do about it. Our cultural conditioning is in two minds about how to survive and transcend trauma: it contains the seeds of our own healing (there is more elevating art and literature and nature and human-kindness than can be experienced in even a thousand lifetimes), but the current economic model that drives information and creative media is addicted to showcasing horror, while the self-help industry fails to recognize that fully embodying its own mission would result in its collapse.

I used to be terrified of everything, because I bought the lie that we lived in hell. Even the peacemakers struggled, sometimes suggesting that our world was a sinking ship, and that our only recourse was to bucket out as much water as we could. What we didn't realize was that the ship had already sunk. The patterns of relationship upon which our divided society was built could not serve us any longer. We had been drowning in mutual enmity for centuries, dragged down by the madness of defining our interests as keeping people out rather than welcoming each other as the kind of gift that would liberate us too. The ship had already sunk, because it was never a seaworthy vessel in the first place.

We needed another boat. Peacemakers are engaged in the task of building another boat. A boat on which a new story can be told. A story that acknowledges that while we may see 15,000 fictionalized murders by the age of 16, we'll see a lot more flowers bloom — if only we would learn to look. John O'Donohue called beauty "the divine embrace"; it's not naivety to believe that beauty will save the world. It already has.

And it will go on saving the world, as long as there are people to enfold themselves within this divine embrace, and begin to take seriously the call to hold the space between the perfection of the present moment, and the brokenness of the day. We don't know if this moment will last, but it is our moment. We not only get to choose what to do with it, but we must.

Spiritual masters teach us that it is not what happens that causes us to suffer, *but the stories we tell about it.* Authentic, life-affirming spirituality does not deny the existence of violence, though it does surely work to transcend the negative effects of violence, and to reduce the amount of violence in the world. It does this by helping human beings, one by one, and in community, to face our own shadows: our fears and wounds, the way we project evil onto "enemies," the temptation to the quick gratification of smacking down our opponents, whether by weaponized drones or Facebook comments, without considering the long-term health of people and the planet. Authentic, life-affirming spirituality invites us to tell the truth about violence — which means sometimes facing painful realities, but also means getting things in proportion. It is being widely argued that we currently live in the least violent time in history, for the average human, and that the empowerment of women, the expansion of democracy, a deepening imagination of empathy, and the revolutions in human rights will continue as part of our spiritual evolution.

Some of us for all of us.

Today's real and painful headlines do not refute the trendlines: the world becomes safer when brave people tell a new story. A story that makes room for everyone to play a part in the evolution of love. The story leads them to resist oppression, and transcend it with a new way of being. They have chosen not to remain the victims of a story that says the world is getting worse. They are the bringers of new light, the willing recipients of the gift of courage in the face of resistance, the bearers of the pain that is and the transcenders of the lie that exaggerates it, the pioneers of what comes next on our journey toward wholeness. And they do this because they know just one thing.

There is a better story.

We're all here together to tell it. ✦

We don't have to look far for examples of the six default-oppositional stories, especially if we get our information from electronic news media. But there are even more examples of the Seventh Story than anyone could possibly know.

Why are we so sure? Perhaps because without the presence of Seventh Story, we might not be here to write about it at all. So influential is the Seventh Story on how any human beings get through even one interaction with another, we take it for granted to the point of not even knowing that it's there. But not noticing it leads to a hugely dangerous problem: when we are asked to tell stories about how the world works, we revert to the six oppositional-default stories, and the myth of redemptive violence. This is what false consciousness really is: believing something that isn't true, and acting on it, despite the fact that our everyday experiences completely contradict the belief. People love each other, help strangers, and don't kill anyone every day. People participate in compassion-oriented activism, works of mercy, reconciliation movements *all the time.*

The problem is not that nonviolence doesn't work, but that *its story hasn't been told.*

In other words, the stories we tell most often, or at least the loudest, are distortions of reality: most of us overestimate the violence and suffering, and undervalue the presence of reconciliation and healing in the world. This is only natural — the real-life car crash or burning building attract the reflexive attention of our reptile brains, just as the fictional car chase or exploding planet do.

Spectacle sells.

Human evolution away from violence, poverty, hunger, illiteracy, gender discrimination and more is a long-term process, of course, but the economic model on which 24/7 news media are based does not lend itself to reflection on the arc of history. Anything but. Anyone who has spent an evening binge-watching *any* mainstream news channel knows that a conversation about, for instance, the eradication of guinea worm, or Scandinavian restorative justice, or the achievements of the peace process in northern Ireland is unlikely. Instead, there is ugliness, portrayed as if it were the core reality of life.

Now this is not to say that we shouldn't talk about violence and suffering — of course not. But if we are to take violence and suffering seriously, we need to treat them *honestly*. No positive purpose will be served by overstating the truth, or confusing headlines with trends.

What would be better would be to take responsibility for learning what is real, based on sources that are accountable to both facts and wisdom. This includes learning, as best we can, how much violence there actually is in the world; seeking to understand its roots and consequences; amplifying stories about how to repair the impact of violence already done; and working to erode the foundations for violence that has not yet occurred.

This means telling stories which expose the myth that

violence redeems; stories which reveal the fatal consequences of beliefs and practices that promote separation and avoidance of suffering; and stories which don't work.

But far more important, and effective: we have to go deeper, for an absence of violence is not the same thing as the Beloved Community, just a step in the right direction. We can dwell *too* much on exposing violence. Thinking about how not to be violent defines itself in terms of its opposite, and we know that oppositional energy always recreates itself. The best way to overcome evil is to do something good. Sometimes we need to focus our energy on resistance or protest, to be sure — but that's more like an emergency appendectomy than a long-term strategy for healing the whole body.

It's better to talk with God than the Devil.

So here are some examples of stories that reveal the failure of oppositional-default narratives, followed by a sketch of how cinema, television, literature, music, politics, religion and culture have invited us into the Seventh Story.

One note: I speak, as everybody does, from a perspective both gifted and limited by where I'm from. I'm a white man who grew up in a Celtic culture, and while I've been blessed to encounter many different peoples along the way, my horizons are just that: horizons. I can only see to the next hill. So what follows, for what it's worth, is a brief sketch of stories that have meant something to me. You will have your own — and that, of course, is part of the beauty given birth to by the Seventh Story: instead of one of us having all the answers, each of us gets to — must — play a role in the mosaic of global and even cosmic understanding. A deeper dive is invited in our online spaces — what stories matter to you?

What I've done here is to give examples of stories that reveal the failure of oppositional-default narratives by inviting us into the Seventh reconciliation story. They are offered as ways into thinking about how life is when we live the six stories, or how it could be if we lived the Seventh.

For poetic integrity, I've offered at least seven examples each. We invite you to learn more about each, and more. The Global Nonviolent Action Database at Swarthmore College is a great place to start.

In POLITICS large and small –

1. The northern Ireland Peace Process (1994-present day) — when people agreed to talk instead of using violence, and determined that sharing power with each other was preferable to winner takes all.

On the day after Pope John Paul II died in 2005, some anti-Catholic graffiti went up on a very conspicuous location in Belfast. It was an opportunity for easy condemnation — of the nastiness of the slogan and the people who wrote it; it also would have been easy to shirk responsibility, and wait for local authorities to clean it up (which would take time during which the damage of the message would be repeated). Instead, a small group of friends went out at four o'clock in the morning, and painted over the graffiti, in large letters, one word that could open the door to a reconciliation path: SORRY.

2. The US Civil Rights Movement (1954-1968) - when oppressed people instead of giving into the fight or flight impulse, but offering a third way: nonviolent resistance that exposes the injustice of the system and invites the oppressor to turn toward the good.

Standing on the shoulders of giants or nurturing the spirits of pioneers such as Ella Baker, Harriet Tubman, Rosa Parks, Fannie Lou Hamer, the Highlander Folk School in New Market, Tennessee, which taught nonviolent organizing, helped thousands of Black people register to vote, and was the site for the adaptation of the song we now know as We Shall Overcome.

3. The nonviolent dimensions of the anti-apartheid movement in South Africa (1960-1994), overturning an oppositional-default story so obvious, it even used the word "separate" in its futility.

When Archbishop Desmond Tutu stepped out of the pulpit of St George's Cathedral in Cape Town, greeting the members of the South African secret police engaged in surveillance of anti-apartheid activists. Refusing to go along with the shadow of secrecy or stir up hatred against them, Tutu invited these men to do the thing that would not only be best for the movement, but might even save their own souls: to take one step forward, join the struggle toward justice for all, and make amends for their shameful behavior.

4. Steps toward peace in Israel and Palestine, where the Parents Circle-Families Forum (1995-present day) gathers people whose loved ones have been killed in political violence.

They facilitate dialogues among opponents, summer camps for kids from both sides of the divide, and even donating blood to each other. The slogan?: "Could you hurt someone who has your blood running through their veins?"

5. Movements that refuse invisibility for the oppressed, and demand that we recognize the equal dignity of all.

The founding in 1962, by César Chávez and Dolores Huerta, of the United Farm Workers of America: an invitation to honor the humanity of those who grow and harvest the food without which our lives would not be possible.

6. Stirrings of consciousness about the responsibility many of us are born into: the fact that our forebears have forced others to pay a price for what we now hold.

The Waitingi Tribunal in Aotearoa New Zealand (1975-present day), which investigates breaches of the treaty between the English Crown and Maori peoples, or the restorative process of un-naming the rock formerly known as Mount McKinley, in which the temporal authorities sought permission, in a good way, from the Alaskan Athabascan people to use instead the sacred and ancient name, Denali. It did not undo the genocide of Native Peoples, but perhaps it is the beginning of making amends.

7. **And the countless people who have seen it as their business to help heal the world from its addiction to misusing power.**

My friend Paul could tell you about a woman he knows who made 2,000 visits to people bereaved through sectarian violence in Ireland; and my friend Mona could tell you about how she responded to attacks on folks who share her religion by giving a way free donuts to anyone would would Talk to a Muslim; or you could visit (or even start) a Share Cafe or Time bank, where skills that people need are exchanged in accessible ways; or Not In Our Town, working to build safe inclusive communities; or the "interrupters" working to Cure Violence in Chicago; or how food that would otherwise be unjustifiably thrown away is used to make tremendous food for anyone who needs it, at no charge, by the 12 Baskets Cafe in Asheville, North Carolina.

In CINEMA –

1. Isabel Coixet's exquisite film ***My Life Without Me*** (2003) in which Sarah Polley responds to a death sentence by serving the invitation of love. It's an echo of an earlier work of Japanese magic, Akira Kurosawa's ***Ikiru*** (1952), the antidote to our unlived lives; which also helped birth Hirokazu-Koreeda's reinvention of the ***After Life*** (1998) by suggesting that eternity is a story we tell. And the choice of story is entirely ours.

2. ***The Fisher King*** (1991) reconciles the superficially competing interests of four fascinating characters — the need for redemption after failure, the need for trust in relationships, the need for restoration after trauma, and the need to be seen — by presenting the Quest for the Holy Grail as a New York tale. In this telling, however, the eternal life granted by the cup is nothing less than the Seventh Story.

3. In ***Babette's Feast*** (1987), a community living under the oppressive regime of isolation and purification finds itself healed by the presence of an artist who has figured out that dividing the world into "them" and "us" may harm "us" most of all. If Babette were curating a banquet of cinematic

community for the common good, she might add ***Queen of Katwe*** (2016), ***Moonlight*** (2016), ***The Station Agent*** (2003), and ***Smoke*** (1995).

4. Along with ***Reds*** (1981) and ***Pride*** (2014), Ava DuVernay's ***Selma*** (2014) brilliantly portrays the challenges of building a social movement — the tensions and costs, alongside the hopes and achievements; and the fact that truly overcoming oppression always offers to liberate the oppressor too. It may not always work, in the short term, as ***Life is Beautiful*** (1997) shows, but nonviolence makes for a better life than the one that just follows orders.

5. For stories about the miracle of the Seventh Story in everyday life, ***Paterson*** (2016) gives us working class life in an industrial city as a kind of utopia; ***The Dam-Keeper*** (2014) speaks to transcending victimization through being vulnerable; ***The Apartment*** (1960) asks us to "shut up and deal" with the call to, finally, love ourselves and each other more than money and reputation; ***Mary and Max*** (2009) evokes friendship as the truest home we have to offer; ***The Accidental Tourist*** (1988) is honest about grief and healing; ***Wonderstruck*** (2017) reminds us that there are, perhaps, millions of people who would be the best friend we've ever had, if only we would let ourselves bump into them; ***Make***

Way for Tomorrow (1937) shows what happens when we don't; and ***The Straight Story*** (1999) says that making amends to those we have harmed is partly about healing ourselves too.

6. Turning to the cosmic, by ***2001: A Space Odyssey*** (1968), ***The Tree of Life*** (2011), ***The Exorcist*** (1973), ***A Matter of Life and Death*** (1946), ***Groundhog Day*** (1993), ***Arrival*** (2016), ***Interstellar*** (2014), ***Fearless*** (1993), we are lifted to look up from our small visions of life, and to see something beyond merely good, but transcendent kindness, a massive backdrop for the small stories we tell, the ground of all being, the notion that love doesn't just conquer all, but invented it.

7. And just to show that you don't have to replicate the myth of redemptive violence in order to attract huge box office, I nominate ***Armageddon*** (1998) as the most Seventh Story blockbuster in the history of blockbusters. You want exciting chases, explosions, and special effects? You got 'em — let's put Bruce Willis in a spaceship. You want a lethal force that needs to be dealt with, creating enough tension to carry a story? Sure, we can have a meteorite threatening all life on earth. And then — you make a fun, silly, BIG movie in which no human harms any other human; in which international collaboration is fundamentally necessary, because the nations

have finally realized that they all face the same danger; in which the climactic act of courage is one person exchanging their life for another, by choice, for the common good, for the sake of love. It can be done — the most popular movies could actually be just as wise as the smartest ones.

In LITERATURE and POETRY –

1. Alice Walker's ***The Color Purple*** (1982) is not the greatest American novel merely because of how it invents a language and credibly reveals the evolution of one human soul over the course of decades. It's the greatest American novel because it manages to both tell the truth about suffering, facing it head-on, at the same time refusing to dehumanize its villains, granting not only the *possibility* of restorative justice rather than vengeance, but its *necessity.*

2 & 3. The Kiwi author, and true friend of the Seventh Story, Mike Riddell, did something similar in his magnificent novel ***The Insatiable Moon*** (1997), in which God shows up in the form of Arthur, an indigent Maori man whom the conventional world calls schizophrenic, mostly because he believes in love. Arthur is a literary cousin of the title character in John Irving's ***A Prayer for Owen Meany*** (1989), which also wants us to ache for when humans treat each other as less-than, and imagine the kind of heroic life devoted to love rather than self.

4, 5 & 6. Wendell Berry's ***Mad Farmer Poems*** (1991, 2014) and Pádraig Ó Tuama's ***Sorry for Your Troubles*** (2013) and

Anne Carson's ***Autobiography of Red*** (1998) are all poetic invitations to imagine the world as it could be, by first facing how it actually is.

7. And the Jesus who appears in ***The Brothers Karamazov*** (1880) understands something profound about how to nonviolently transcend the principalities and powers that think they rule the world: we are invited to speak what we feel, not what we ought to say.

In TELEVISION –

1, 2, 3 & 4. ***Northern Exposure*** (1990-1995) wherein all the eccentric people you've ever met seem to have moved to the same small Alaska town, face the struggles and embrace the joys of everyday life, and see the magic everywhere. A crockpot, a melting pot, a delicious stew that tastes wonderful. Smaller-scale wonders are to be found in ***Detectorists*** (2014-2017), wherein all the eccentric people you've ever met seem to have moved to the same small English town, face the struggles and embrace the joys of everyday life, and see the magic everywhere. Both *Northern Exposure* and *Detectorists,* along with ***The Muppet Show*** (1976-1981) and ***The Good Place*** (2016-continuing), do something miraculous: they show that cooperative community, serving the common good, and experiencing love, doesn't take a miracle at all.

5 & 6. Two nonfiction series have stayed with me for long enough that I can't leave them off this list: ***The Mind Traveler*** (1998), in which the neurologist Oliver Sacks invested lovely time with folks whose brilliant brains were used against them by a society afraid of its own shadow; and Michael Palin's delightful travel documentaries, beginning with ***Around the***

World in 80 Days (1989), for two reasons: of course there is the encounter with people and land, but also the way Palin allows himself to be unsure of himself, which of course is the only way to ever go somewhere new.

7. The single greatest television drama I have ever seen is ***Rectify*** (2013-2016), about a man released pending a new trial after nineteen years on death row. Not only an investigation of the literal imperfections — and worse — enacted by retributive notions of justice, but a slow-burning exploration of the interior journey of one man who contains monumental suffering, and discovers courageous love not just despite the suffering, but probably because of it.

In NONFICTION –

1. Personal reflections on how life actually works: ***The Hour of Land*** by Terry Tempest Williams (on how the US National Parks system is a microcosm of the gift of, and the amends that need made because of, the nation's self-perception); ***Hope in the Dark*** by Rebecca Solnit (which reminds us that the past is not the story of violence triumphing, but of nonviolence healing), and ***The Cloister Walk*** by Kathleen Norris (in which a life is changed by standing still).

2. Works of political, sociological, and philosophical reflection on the past, inviting a vision of the future: ***Honest Patriots: Loving a Country Enough to Remember Its Misdeeds*** by Donald W Shriver, ***The More Beautiful World Our Hearts Know is Possible*** by Charles Eisenstein, and ***Saving Paradise*** by Rita Nagashima Brock and Rebecca Parker.

3. New visions of memory, that upend what we think we know: Steven Pinker's ***The Better Angels of our Nature: Why Violence Has Declined***, which tells the astonishing story hiding in plain sight: that humans have been hurting each other less; and ***Human Smoke: The Beginnings of World War II, the End of Civilization***, which challenges us to recognize that people

have always proposed credible methods to reduce violence: the question is whether or not we are willing to listen.

4. On the history and practice of Seventh Story nonviolence: ***Lost Prophet: The Life and Times of Bayard Rustin*** by John D'Emilio, ***Moving Beyond Sectarianism*** by Joseph Liechty and Cecelia Clegg, ***A Force More Powerful: A Century of Nonviolent Conflict*** by Peter Ackerman and Jack DuVall, ***Speak Peace in a World of Conflict*** by Marshall Rosenberg, ***Martin Luther King, The Inconvenient Hero*** by Vincent Harding, and ***Gandhi on Non-Violence***, edited by Thomas Merton.

5. On what life is really about, and personally transformative practices that will bring ourselves into greater alignment with it: ***A Mind at Home with Itself*** by Byron Katie and Stephen Mitchell, ***Coming Back to Life*** by Joanna Macy and Molly Young Brown, ***The Soul's Code*** by James Hillman, and ***Living an Examined Life*** by James Hollis.

6. Turning to the cosmic, and its relationship with the mundane: no book has shaped me more than Walter Wink's ***The Powers that Be***, his groundbreaking illustration of power, violence, and active spirituality. It's in a category of its own. Whether prayer has ever meant something to you, or you

have always been skeptical, consider it.

7. And finally, what might seem like a mischievous choice: Marie Kondo's ***The Life-Changing Magic of Tidying Up***. Why? Because the environment we control is both a manifestation of our inner life, and fuel for it. Kondo's two simple principles could guide each of us to make the world better for everyone. Do you need it? Does it bring you joy to have it?

In RELIGION & CULTURE –

1, 2, 3 & 4. Learning the stories of the **Buddha**'s response to his own poisoning, or the **Taizé** community's to the murder of their founder Brother Roger, or the **Mennonite martyr Dirk Willems**, executed after rescuing his oppressor from drowning. or how, day after day, people everywhere practice the truth that you cannot love God without loving your neighbor, and you cannot love your neighbor without loving yourself.

5, 6 & 7. Or we could visit Medellín, Colombia, where **Fernando Botero**, one of the most acclaimed contemporary artists donated priceless sculptures to be placed on city streets in the belief that public spaces should be made more beautiful than functional; we could join the **Peace One Day movement**, calling for an annual 24 hour ceasefire in all the world's violent conflicts; we could pay attention to the **Singing Revolution** which used the power of music to help bring down an oppressive regime in Estonia. We could consider the many spaces in which conventional scarcity economics are being replaced with **offering folks the chance to pay whatever they can afford** to participate.

In MUSIC –

1 & 2. We could start with Stevie Wonder's ***Songs in the Key of Life*** or Beyoncé's ***Lemonade***, remembering that the struggle for justice depends on facing the truth, but reveling in beauty, too.

3 & 4. Or reflect on the gentle laments and hopes to do better in David Wilcox & Nance Pettit's Rumi album ***Out Beyond Ideas***, or Peter Gabriel's ***So***, ***Us***, and ***Up***.

5. You could listen to anything David Byrne has recorded, while reading his inspirational website **Reasons to be Cheerful**.

6 & 7. And then, and then, and then…if you really want your mind and body to slow down long enough to become the antidote to what Blaise Pascal once said is the cause of all the problems in the world, you could sit still in a chair for ten minutes (or more), and listen, really listen, to ***The Lark Ascending*** by Ralph Vaughan Williams and ***A Love Supreme*** by John Coltrane, two works whose entire reason for being is simply this: to remind us that we are not the protagonists of the world, and that we will best find our fit there by amplifying the story of love, and diving right in. ✦

5

The Seventh Story in Context

Brian D. McLaren

According to our best current estimate, the story we find ourselves in began 13.8 billion years ago.

That number boggles the mind, so let's reduce the scale to a more manageable number. Taking the lead from the evolutionary thinker Michael Dowd, let's imagine that we could shrink down 13.8 billion years to 100 years. In that framework, each day would cover about 400,000 years, each hour, about 17,000 years, each minute about 278 years, and each second about 4.5 years.

What we call the Big Bang — or the Big Bloom, if you prefer — happens at 12:00 am on day 1. On day 2, hydrogen comes into being. It isn't until years 25-30 that more complex atoms like carbon or oxygen form.

Around year 67, our solar system takes shape, and in year 69, our beautiful planet solidifies in its orbit around the sun. Sometime during year 71, Earth comes alive, as simple life forms develop in the oceans. The next year, some of those simple life forms acquire the ability to draw energy from the sun through photosynthesis. They begin producing oxygen as a byproduct, which oxygenates the atmosphere and makes possible the development of animal life on land. For the next 25 years, life diversifies and fills available niches in the oceans, on land, and in the air.

Fast forward to May of year 98, and the first dinosaurs appear. They are Earth's dominant advanced life form until July of 99, when a huge asteroid strikes earth and causes mass extinctions.

Between July and December, mammals proliferate. Then, around December 24 of year 99, hominids, our ancient ancestors, appear among the mammals. On December 25, they begin using stone tools, and on December 29, they learn to use fire.

On the morning of December 31, early humans develop language, and around 11:20 pm, they begin to develop what we think of as civilization.

Everything we know about human history and culture happens in these final minutes of this last day of the last year of our one-hundred-year story.

Early in our development, our biggest threats might have been predators like lions, tigers, wolves, and bears, along with unexpected events like droughts, floods, earthquakes, and fires. But before long, the greatest threats that humans faced were other humans.

Some enemies were external, part of other bands, tribes, city-states, or kingdoms. Other enemies were neighbors, members of the same tribe who became rivals, thieves, killers, grudge-holders, or oppressors.

To deal with the threats posed by fellow humans, our ancestors developed a growing arsenal of weapons, from rocks to clubs to spears to knives to swords to arrows to poisons to guns to artillery to bombs to chemical, biological, and nuclear weapons. In addition, they developed methods of government, law enforcement, war, propaganda, punishment, and torture.

They employed their arsenal of violence reduction techniques through one larger social strategy: domination. Usually domination involved elevating one alpha male to a position of privilege. From that position, he would keep subordinate males in submission, creating pyramids of hierarchy with men over women, the old over the young, the rich over the poor, enslavers over slaves, and kings, nobles, priests, and their associates over others. In exchange for maintaining order, the patriarch was usually given access to exceptional privileges, from wealth to sex to social deference and even worship.

Exceptionally ambitious or violent alpha males would lead their tribe or city-state to dominate not only in their group but beyond it, subjugating their neighbors to genocide, slavery, exploitation, or assimilation, and ruling over larger numbers of people and greater expanses of land. These nations, empires, and superpowers would recount their history as a heroic narrative of domination.

Of course, dominated people would recount the same history as a tragic narrative of oppression. They would dream of getting revenge, of rebelling against their dominators, and of replacing them as the dominant group. They would frame their lives by a narrative of revolution.

When problems, tensions, divisions, and anxieties simmered in a group, a majority would often find a minority to blame and scapegoat. They would live by a purification narrative, leading to oppression, exclusion, or genocide of the minority.

When possible, oppressed or scapegoated groups would flee the hostile conditions posed by domination, revolution, and purification narratives. They would seek to withdraw to an isolated place to live in peace. This isolation narrative hastened the spread of humans to every habitable niche around the planet.

Rather than geographically isolating, some individuals and families sought to create their own zones of safety and comfort by accumulating land, wealth, and power. This accumulation narrative created privileged elites who sought to live above the fray.

Those unable to achieve or maintain dominance, enforce purification, flee for safety in a new place, or accumulate enough wealth, land, and power to feel safe were left as vulnerable victims. Within their victimization narrative, the disinherited or powerless could only hope for pity or some magical or divine intervention to reverse their fortunes.

These six narratives — domination, revolution, purification, isolation, accumulation, and victimization — have been driving forces in human history at least since about 11:20 pm on December 31. At about 11:59:44, human capacity for violence took a major turn with the first deployment of nuclear weapons. A second or two later, the demands humans made on the planet's ecosystems exceeded the capacity of the planet to sustain them long-term, unleashing a series of mutually-intensifying environmental crises.

Since that time, our species has had to contemplate the real possibility of its own self-sabotage or even self-annihilation as the outcome of its primary stories.

Around the margins, another narrative has been taking shape during these most recent moments of our hundred-year history. In this narrative, humans envision learning to live in harmony with one another and with the boundary conditions (or laws) of nature. We imagine seeing all our fellow humans — and all living things — as part of one family of relations, sharing in the same unfolding story or song of creation. We imagine ourselves creating conditions in which peace and well-being are not only possible but normal, and in which inevitable conflicts can be resolved through justice, kindness, wisdom, and love.

Instead of *us over them* (domination), *us overcoming them* (revolution), *us rejecting them* (purification), *us apart from them* (isolation), *us under them* (victimization) or *us hoarding from them* (accumulation), we imagine us and them as part of one larger us. We imagine "us" reconciling with "them", us working with them for the common good, us seeking to understand them as our sisters and brothers; we even allow for the possibility that we are invited to live with the earth itself, not in exploitation, but in partnership.

As the amazing 13.8 billion-year story of the cosmos continues to unfold, in this little corner of the universe, we hope to live and tell a story of justice and joy, love and peace, for the benefit of future generations who will be born into the story that there is no them at all. ✦

6

What Now?

Gareth Higgins

The green around the house is lush, and the rain this morning makes it lusher, and I love it.

However, in my mind today it's not just lush green, nor mildly heavy rain, reminding me of how life has been here long before me, or the news, or anything else. Today is also filled with trouble for so many people.

But Frederick Buechner says, "Here is the world. Beautiful and terrible things will happen. Do not be afraid."

And John O'Donohue says, "The duty of privilege is absolute integrity."

And WB Yeats says, "Tread softly because you tread on my dreams."

And Alice Walker says, "Hope to sin only in the service of waking up."

And Byron Katie says, "Everyone's in love with me, even if they don't know it yet." (Or words to that effect.) What if everyone loved you? What if you walked into a room thinking that? Or never believed the thought, "They don't get me?" Liberation!

And Viktor Frankl says it's not what happens to you that is the cause of your suffering, but how you think about it.

It's raining, and the green is lush.

How to live, knowing the pain, and the joy, and the power, and the lack?

How to even think about the pain in the world without being egotistical, without making it about me?

In *The Exorcist,* the wise and resilient priest Father Lankester Merrin says that cruelty and horror tends to make us think ourselves unlovable, unworthy of goodness, hopeless — as if we were magnets for only the ugly. Thinking ourselves ugly, we treat others as if they deserved nothing better. And so evil recycles itself.

So in our response to cruelty, to horror, there must be more love, more kindness, more joy at the lush green. Not indulgence, not selfishness, but gratitude-becoming-action.

The duty of privilege is absolute integrity.

I have a responsibility to evaluate my own power, and lack, use the power for the common good, and the lack as the place from which I ask for help.

Byron Katie responded to a question along the lines of, "Well what should we do about the injustice in the world?" with "The most that we can."

The Seventh Story is a space that invites us to transform the horror in the world and the pain in our own lives, experiencing the vastly greater gifts of the world, and using the gifts in our lives. It's a space where we can see the forest **and** the trees. Lush green. ✦

7

A Seventh Story Manifesto

Gareth Higgins & Brian D. McLaren

What's happening is not just happening *to* us, although it may feel like that. We are either participating *in* it, or acting *on* it.

So the public figure who appears to us as either a rampaging monster, or a warrior-savior, depending on the perspective granted by the power we hold (or don't), and our orientation towards other people, the planet, and our values, in the deepest sense is only able to be either by our consent.

And we don't mean electoral consent, or at least not only that — we mean the consent of our minds and hearts, the time we have given over to him, in fealty, or in opposition.

Something we must take seriously about the intensity and aggression in the current moment is how easy, how natural it is to be provoked to anger, despair, and even trauma. One unintended consequence is that when we are caught up in the drama, or sometimes the horror show, we distract ourselves from being actors *in* it.

If we recognize this, important questions can emerge:

What am I going to do with my place in the world, with my power, and with my lack?

What contribution will I make to the common good?

What am I willing to give up?

When will I ask for help?

Because, truly, help is available.

*

And so, with that in mind, we invite you to join us in a movement for the Seventh Story, co-creating a better world for everyone, including the world itself.

We suggest five insights that might help unlock us from the six stories of separation, selfishness, and scapegoating.

1: Humans initially desire things not because we actually want them, but because *our rivals* want them.

Notice your desires, and when possible, name them, and remember your power to say "yes," "no," or "not right now" to the demands they make of you.

2: Jesus's life and death were not an invitation to more scapegoating, but the end of it.

Devote yourself to the example and teachings of our greatest moral leaders and visionaries who summon us to a way of life that promotes the good of people and the earth. Start with those of your own culture or religion, but don't stop there. Pay special attention to the wisdom of indigenous traditions.

3: Becoming fully human involves defecting from mimetic rivalry, and from the notion that anyone else should ever be my scapegoat.

Avoid blaming, scapegoating, insulting, or shaming anyone, remembering that even the people who bother you most are your neighbors.

4: One way to prevent war is to give preemptive gifts to our enemies.

Show kindness rather than vengeance and generosity rather than judgment to your enemies or opponents.

5: These can be profoundly difficult and complex ideas, but there is simplicity on the other side of complexity, summed up universal wisdom:

Devote yourself to Love.

Love your neighbor.

Love yourself.

Love the earth.

Love the Spirit of Love that fills the universe.

The first and last step: do unto others as you would have them do unto you, and don't do unto others what you would not want them to do to you.

This wisdom has always been true, but it finds expression in different ways, depending on the personal, social, and cultural context. Many of us are so immersed in the six stories of separation, selfishness, and scapegoating that some decisive action is required. We invite you to the following commitments (and we can practice them together — follow us online and join in):

1: Pay attention. Alongside considering the wider world, pay attention to your soul, your neighborhood, your local and regional stories, and find others who do the same. Nurture your personal wellbeing and that of your community, otherwise you will neither thrive in a challenging world, nor be useful to the service of the common good.

2: Don't pay attention. Don't fund the six stories of separation, selfishness, and scapegoating: withhold your attention and the money you steward from **any** media outlet or public figure that uses fear to build an audience. Boycott media sources whose editorial vision and economic model depend on replicating the six stories; and give your attention to those who seek to lead with the seventh story of reconciliation. In other words: when you encounter any entity that believes in the old adage "if it bleeds, it leads," switch off and look elsewhere.

3: Seek mentors who will help you discern a personal sense of calling to the common good. Your gift is connected to your wound, and the world's great need. Serving from the place where these three — the gift, the wound, and the need — intersect is the best way to heal yourself, and offer healing to others.

4: Tell the truth. In a world of competing information sources, seek wisdom above propaganda. Enlarge your frame: see the whole world as your home. Learn the difference between headlines and trendlines.

5: Learn spiritual practices that heal and offer resilience: the could include clearings, accountability, shadow work.

6: Open yourself to seeing things through "the eyes of the other". Seek a friendship with someone who whom you disagree politically. Look for things to praise in others, even when they vote differently. Learn about building equitable community in which everyone has a fair stake. Don't contribute to polarization.

7: **Join or help start a circle** of friends committed to the Seventh Story. Don't journey alone. Encourage others to do the same.

Seventh Story Circles

We know that for humans to thrive, we need four things: food, water, air, and shelter. We tend to define shelter as walls and a roof, but there's far more to shelter than that.

In the community we call *The Porch*, we're exploring the idea that shelter also includes three components that most of us lack: **a sense of purpose** for the common good; an **elder wisdom figure or mentor** who can help advise, inspire, and offer feedback; and **a close circle of friends** who share stories, gifts and needs.

Some of us have been meeting in such circles, and are finding that they help heal the epidemic of loneliness, spiritual emptiness, and the general heaviness that seems to dominate public conversation these days. Want to try it for yourself? We invite you to form **a Seventh Story Circle**, wherever you are, and to use the simple format below to build it.

For the circle, we encourage the following:

Gather at least two other people, and no more than eight in total. It's great to have some age diversity in the group if possible — especially to invite the presence of wise elders as well as enthusiastic people who are earlier on their journey. Invite them to meet once — just once to see how it goes — with the following format:

Pick a time to meet for lunch, or coffee, or dinner at someone's house; or if you're meeting virtually, to do so by video call. Make the food simple — potluck is great.

Have someone facilitate by leading the questions — and you can rotate this from week to week.

Open with words like:

"This is **a Seventh Story Circle,** in which we seek to build community, deepen our life's purpose, share our needs, and live better. Everyone is welcome. We'll have two rounds of simple questions, and everyone is invited to speak from the heart. We honor confidentiality in this circle — what is said here, stays here, unless we have received the consent of the person to share their story. We use "I" statements — speaking about our own experience, gifts, and needs. We don't interrupt each other, and we also respect each other's time, by seeking to be concise in our responses. We commit to the common good, to learning the ways of love, in the spirit of sitting on a porch with a wise elder, knowing that we are not alone, someone has already been where we are, and that kindness is waiting around every corner. All it takes is for someone to go first."

Now we will have our first round of questions. Everyone is invited to respond to each of the first three questions, with each person responding to all three before moving to the next person. We invite a response of up to two minutes for each question. (Agree someone to be timekeeper, and to offer a gentle nudge when the time is up. You can take longer if it works for the group, especially if it has a smaller number of people in it.)

1: What is bringing me life?

2: What is challenging, draining, or deadening me?

3: We are intrigued by the story that the purpose of life is to devote ourselves to love, and to do to and with others what we would like them to do to and with us. We are awakening to the reality that there is no "them and us," there is only us.

In light of this, what is one opportunity I have had since we last met to live this story, and what did I do with that opportunity? What did I learn from it? What would I like to do differently next time? What is an upcoming opportunity I know I will have to live this story, and what would I like to do with it?

After everyone has had the chance to respond to each of the three questions, ask the final question of the whole group:

4: Having heard what we have heard, is there anyone who would like to ask for something from the group, and is there anyone who would like to offer something to anyone in the group?

(This can be as practical as "I need a babysitter," as profound as "I am having an existential crisis and would like someone to go for a walk with me once a week for the next month," or as radical as "I can't pay my rent right now, could the group help support me until I get on my feet?")

The rest is up to you. We'd love to hear how it goes — so please contact us to let us know if you're interested in starting a circle where you live. ✦

www.theseventhstory.com

Who are the children of the future? I should like to answer: the people who renounce domination and the dreams of rule, people who are not victorious and to not dream of victories, but who open themselves and their institutions in creative receptivity towards what is divine, towards what is human, and towards what is natural. These people are the heirs of the future.

–Juergen Moltmann

We're grateful to many friends helped with the shaping of the ideas in this book, and we look forward to continued conversations.

From Gareth: *to the friends who enlarge my circle of belonging, courage, and reconciliation, and especially Brian Ammons.*

From Brian: *to my five grandchildren: Averie, Ella, Mia, Lucas, and Ada. I hope the seventh story will guide your life.*

This book is a companion to *Cory and the Seventh Story*,
a children's fable about "them" and "us."

We invite you to learn more at
www.theseventhstory.com

Notes

On Jan 24 2021 Letitia Jensen gave us this book as a gift. Hank finished it on Jan 26 2021.